THE NATIONAL TRUS

MW00681976

The Prehistoric Monuments of
AVEBURY

WILTSHIRE

CAROLINE MALONE   MA, PhD Cantab, MIFA

Lecturer in Archaeology, University of Bristol
Formerly Inspector of Ancient Monuments and Curator
of the Alexander Keiller Museum, Avebuty

Avebury stone circle is over 4000 years old. It is one of the largest pre-historic henges in Britain and, like Stonehenge, it has been designated as a World Heritage Site. The monuments of the Avebury area are held in guardianship for the nation by English Heritage and are managed by the National Trust, which owns much of the surrounding land. This detailed and authoritative account of Avebury's ceremonial sites, ancient avenues and barrows has been written by a former curator of the Keiller Museum at Avebury, where many of the prehistoric finds, tools and pottery discovered during excavations are displayed.

CONTENTS

Unless otherwise stated illustrations are copyright English Heritage and the photographs were taken by the English Heritage Photographic Section

Archaeological terms used in the text are explained in the glossary on page 55

First published 1990, second edition 1994, reprinted 1995, 1997, 1998, 2000, 2001, 2002, 2003, 2006 (twice), 2007

Printed in England by Acculith 76 for National Trust (Enterprises) Ltd,
Heelis, Kemble Drive, Swindon, Wiltshire SN2 2NA
ISBN 978 184359 270 9

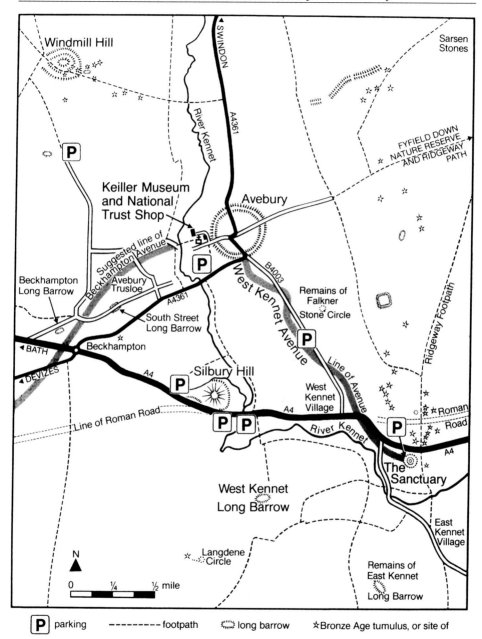

P parking   ---------- footpath   🔆 long barrow   ✶Bronze Age tumulus, or site of

TOUR AND DESCRIPTION

Introduction

The monuments of Neolithic Avebury form one of the most complete prehistoric complexes in Europe.

The **Avebury Circle** (*c*2600–2100BC) is one of the largest henges in Britain. The monument, although undated by modern dating methods, was probably constructed between the first and second phases of Stonehenge (3100 and 2100BC), and is roughly contemporary with the henges of Durrington Walls and Woodhenge. Unlike Stonehenge, the local Sarsen stones of the Avebury Circles are of natural unworked stone.

The earliest monument in the complex is **Windmill Hill**, which was first occupied in *c*3700BC, during the Earlier Neolithic. The enclosures of the causewayed 'camp' were constructed *c*3250BC, and are contemporary with the earliest constructions at **The Sanctuary.**

The **West Kennet Long Barrow** (*c*3700–3500BC), is one of the largest and best-preserved chambered tombs in Britain. It was in use for over 1000 years.

Despite the detailed excavations at **Silbury Hill** (2700BC), the purpose of the largest man-made mound in Europe remains a mystery.

The **West Kennet Avenue** of standing stones (*c*2300–2000BC) was constructed as a ceremonial route linking the Avebury Circles with the structures at the Sanctuary.

The **Alexander Keiller Museum** at Avebury forms the interpretative centre of the complex. It contains many exciting finds and displays from excavations at Avebury and provides a graphic history of the monuments.

Avebury Circles
(OS Ref SU 103700)

The surviving parts of the Avebury Circles are largely reconstructed, and the most spectacular sections are those on the western half. However, to appreciate the scale and complexity, visitors should walk around the whole circle. This is naturally divided into four quadrants by the modern roads, and each section is called a sector.

Suggested route
Starting from the western entrance in the High Street (opposite the path from the main car park), follow the track towards the Great Barn and Alexander Keiller Museum, and take the steps up to the **North-west Sector**. Follow the stones around the perimeter towards the great Swindon Stone beside the road. Follow the fenced footpath along the road, and cross over to the **North-east Sector**. Visit the Cove at the centre of the now ruined North Circle, and then either cross over the circle to the far corner, or climb the bank and follow it to the eastern causeway. Cross over Green Street and climb the bank into the **South-east Sector**, and follow the bank round to the Southern Causeway. Descend, and either cross the road to the West Kennet Avenue or walk to the Stones of the Southern Circle and the Obelisk. Then leave the Circle by the gate and cross the road into the **South-west Sector**. Follow the stones along the perimeter to the barber-surgeon stone (the sixth remaining stone from either end), and then leave the sector from the gate into the High Street.

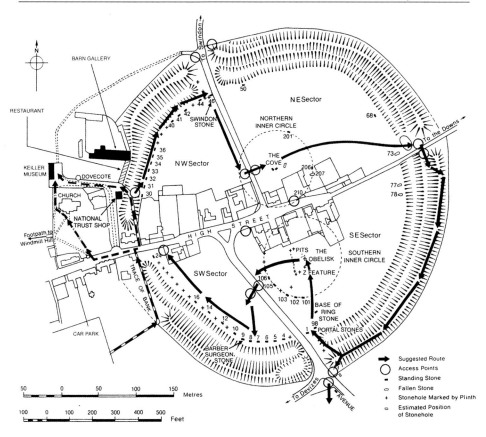

Destruction of the henge

Probably erected *c*2600-2400BC, the great circles and ditch of the Avebury henge remained intact and unused throughout the later prehistoric periods. Roman material found in the upper levels of the ditch suggests that the site may have been visited as a curiosity. During the early Saxon period, from *c*600AD, a settlement was located both inside and just outside the henge. A 'grubenhaus' or long house was found under the present car park, and within the henge, the site may have been a conveniently secure place for a semi-fortified settlement. The Saxons called it *Weala-dic*, meaning

'moat of the British', but the first historical record is in the Assize rolls of 1289. Long before that time, the original Saxon church had been built, a small Benedictine priory on the site of the Manor in 1114, and an oratory in 1180. The church was much enlarged in the late twelfth century and the fine carved font put into position. This refurbishment may correspond with a church revival that successfully suppressed the lingering pagan beliefs which survived in Avebury until the thirteenth century AD. The names of many of the Avebury stones refer to the Devil. The Devil's Chair is the portal stones, and the Cove is the Devil's

Avebury, as it might have appeared some 4500 years ago

Brandirons. The stone chambered tomb at Clatford is the Devil's Den, and the Beckhampton Cove the Devil's Quoits. It would appear that local pagan belief became entangled with Christianity, and that, to appease the Church, the pagan stones were systematically buried in deep pits where the stones stood. All the pottery found under the stones dates from before the early fourteenth century, indicating that the first destruction of Avebury took place during the medieval period. The evidence of the medieval barber-surgeon, crushed under one of the stones, suggests that stone felling was a communal activity for the local population.

Rediscovery of Avebury

Avebury was first recognised as a prehistoric site by the antiquarian John Aubrey in 1649, who discovered it whilst hunting. He wrote that he 'was wonderfully surprised at the sight of those vast stones of which I had never heard before'. Over the following years he recorded many details about the site for his famous, but unpublished, *Monumenta Britannica*. King Charles II heard of the site, and, accompanied by Aubrey, visited it on his way to Bath in 1663. He commanded Aubrey to dig to see if he could find bones. Aubrey, however, did not dig, but speculated instead on the ancient Britons who built Avebury, 'let us imagine what kind of countrie this was in the time of the ancient Britons . . . they were two or three degrees I suppose, less savage than the Americans'. Aubrey's appreciation of a primitive prehistoric Britain was the earliest account of what had until then been a mixture of fantasy and classical mythology. He considered Avebury to be the premier ancient site in Britain, and wrote that 'it does as much exceed in greatness the so reknowned Stonehenge, as a cathedral doeth a parish Church'.

Some sixty years later, from 1719 to 1724, Avebury was again the focus of antiquarian study, when William Stukeley, doctor and clergyman, came to Avebury to study and record the place. He described in similar glowing terms, 'that stupendous temple . . . at Abury . . . the most august work at this day upon the globe of the earth'. During the intervening years, between Aubrey and Stukeley, Avebury had been massively damaged by local builders, breaking the stones and dragging them from their original sockets. The stones were broken into pieces by lighting large straw fires around them and pouring cold water on to the heated stones to crack them. This had devastated the previously well-preserved circles. Stukeley arrived at a time when the village within the circle was growing rapidly, and larger and

An Abury Alto 00 fo. May 20. 1724.

William Stukeley's sketch of stone-burning at Avebury in 1724. The stones were cracked by burning straw in a large pit and were split open with sledge hammers (Bodleian Library)

better-built houses were required. Many of the stone buildings, houses, church, manor and field walls, were built of the broken stones. Stukeley recorded in detail where the stones had been and wrote 'Since I frequented the place, I fear it has suffer'd; but at that time there was scarce a single stone in the original plot wanting, but I could trace it to the person then living who demolish'd it, and to what use and where.'

Stukeley recorded the last picture of an Avebury already much ruined with building and cultivation before it was utterly devastated. However, his interpretation of the ancient stones became romantic and focused on druids and classical gods. He saw himself as a druid, he called the West Kennet Barrow the 'Archdruid's barrow', and considered the great complex to be part of a vast snake, its head at the Sanctuary, and its tail at the end of the Beckhampton Avenue. He altered his measurements and plans to fit his ideas, and, in so doing, provided the foundations for much of the more speculative 'archaeology' of today.

The latter years of the eighteenth century and most of the nineteenth saw little systematic work done at Avebury. Theorists of all types used the now well-published data that Stukeley had produced. Some regarded Avebury as a temple, others as a great burial ground, still others as part of a huge druidical complex, and as an astronomical calendar. The antiquarians Colt Hoare and Cunnington mapped it in 1812, and wrote 'the supposed parent of Stonehenge, the wonder of Britain, and the most interesting and ancient relic of which our island can produce'. Excavations by many interested antiquarians attempted to find evidence of what the great henge was. However, it was not until the archaeologist Harold St George

Avebury, showing its setting in the surrounding landscape

Gray came to Avebury in 1908, as part of his study of stone circles, that systematic excavation took place. Gray concentrated on the great ditch of Avebury, and sank several deep trenches to the bottom, up to 9 m (30 ft) in depth. He discovered that the site was Neolithic and had been dug with antler picks and rakes. He recognised several layers of stratified soil in the ditch, and was able to provide a phasing scheme using the different types of pottery found.

A Skyscan balloon photograph, commissioned by English Heritage

However, it was not until Alexander Keiller actually purchased the site of Avebury and part of the West Kennet Avenue that the stones were properly investigated. Keiller, inspired by Stukeley's account of the Avenue, began excavation and restoration along the Avenue in 1934-35. Stones were located, excavated, and put back into their original positions. Work began in the Circle in the north-west sector in 1937. After clearing the ditch and removing the trees, sometimes

Re-erecting one of the huge sarsen stones at Avebury in 1938

was in the 1930s, had not Keiller undertaken his imaginative programme of restoration.

Description

The **Avebury Stone Circles** are the largest in Britain, located in the third largest henge. In all, the surrounding bank and ditch and the area enclosed cover 11.5 ha (28.5 acres). The site is on a natural chalk dome, sloping gently from the centre. The bank and ditch are 1.3 km (0.8 mile) in length, and were of spectacular scale when first constructed in the mid third millennium BC. At its deepest point, the ditch is about 9 m (30 ft), although this is now filled with silt eroded from the bank. The bank once stood to a maximum of 6.7 m (18 ft) in height, although it is lower today. In all, the span between ditch base and bank crest would have been about 15 m (50 ft), a stunning sight in its original white chalk state. The quarrying methods used

using explosives to shift the great stumps, careful excavation located the buried stones. Where stones had been removed in the seventeenth and eighteenth centuries vast burning pits were discovered, and concrete plinths were positioned where the stones had once stood. The work of excavation and restoration continued in the south-west sector in 1938, and in the southern circle in the southeast sector in 1939.

The work was unique and it restored the ruined site to some of its former glory. Keiller was an innovator, using the latest methods and gadgetry to fulfil his vision of Avebury. The bulk of the stones standing today were excavated and re-erected during the five years of excavation. It is arguable that Avebury would still be the almost unknown site that it

North-west Sector Stones 30–33

North-west Sector: Stone 46 in foreground. The photograph was taken before the trees were felled following Dutch elm disease in the 1970s. Significantly, the church is sited outside the 'pagan' circle

antler picks and rakes, ox-shoulder blades and probably wooden shovels and baskets. The technique appears to have been to sink pits through the hard middle chalk into the softer, tabular lower chalk at intervals along the length of the ditch. Teams may have then quarried at a working face along the length of the ditch, leaving nearly vertical sides and a flat base. This excavation technique varied considerably from that of the Earlier Neolithic henge ditches, where small sections were dug out in 2-3 m (6-9 ft) lengths, leaving small baulks between the sections. Earlier ditches (Windmill Hill and along the West Kennet Long Barrow) were V-shaped in section. The earlier technique may have been the result of small and separate groups undertaking the work, whereas the massive scale of the Avebury ditch suggests that permanent teams would

have been employed in its construction.

Enclosed within the bank and ditch were 98 standing stones about 6.5 m (22 ft) from the perimeter of the ditch. They varied in length from 3 m to 6 m (9 ft-19 ft), and weighed up to 20 tonnes each. In addition there were 27 stones around the North Circle, 29 stones around the South Circle and 12 stones in the west half of the Z-feature.

The dimensions of the Avebury Circle are:

Total area	11.5 ha (28.5 acres)
Depth of ditch	7-10 m (21-30 ft)
Height of bank	6.7 m (18 ft)
Width of ditch (top)	21.3 m (61 ft)
Diameter of ditch	347.5 m (1140 ft)
Circumference of ditch	1353 m (4439 ft)
Width of entrances	15.3 m (50 ft)

It is thought that as much as 1.5 million man-hours would have been needed to construct the bank and ditch and transport the sarsen stones.

The monument has been dated to *c*2600–2100BC on the evidence of the pottery types found (Windmill Hill, Mortlake, Peterborough and Beaker). Phases of construction are not known, but the outer circle, including the Ring Stone, may well have been a late addition. There were two ceremonial avenues: the West Kennet Avenue (100 pairs of stones), entering the south causeway; and the Beckhampton Avenue, entering the west causeway.

The **North-west Sector** was the first to be excavated by Keiller in 1937. Few stones were visible, and the area had become a squalid village rubbish tip covered in trees. Writing in 1939, Keiller described 'the conditions of indescribable squalor and neglect prevailing over most of the area . . . indeed the tangle of rusty pig-wire, the accumulations, to a depth of nearly 3 feet of old tins and broken bottles, around two of the standing stones, to say nothing of the refuse heaps which filled the ditch almost flush with its edges, constituted ungenerously towards rendering the once majestic site of Avebury what it had been for centuries, the outstanding archaeological disgrace of Britain'.

The sector had been much damaged over the centuries, with the levelling of much of the bank behind the Great Barn

North-west Sector: The great Swindon Stone (46) marks the northern entrance

Northern Inner Circle: the two standing stones of the central Cove

in the late seventeenth century. Only four stones were standing, and four more were just visible under old field walls. The remaining stones had been either removed or buried during the medieval period. Divided by the modern road, the northern inner circle had projected into the north-west sector, its remaining stones being recorded by Stukeley in the early eighteenth century before their final destruction. The present outer ring was excavated and the stones placed again in their original post-sockets by Keiller. Several stones had been badly damaged during the eighteenth-century destruction, and efforts were made to piece broken stones together. The much-mended Stone 42 is an example of this work. Nearest the road is the great Swindon Stone, one of the few that has never fallen. Like the massive Portal stones

guarding the southern causeway entrance, this stone, weighing *c* 64.5 tonnes, probably provided a symbolic block to the northern causeway entrance.

The **North-east Sector** has received little systematic research, with a few trenches dug by Smith and Cunnington in 1865 and investigations by Gray in the immediate area of the Cove during his work at Avebury. The sector has few stones visible today, but once contained the bulk of the Northern Circle, 98 m (320 ft) in diameter. This had at least one ring of stones, 27 in number (of which only four survive today), and possibly a smaller circle inside surrounding the central Cove. Originally formed of three stones, the Cove may have been roughly aligned on the moon's most northerly rising point. Stukeley called it the Luna Circle. The stones used were some of the

Southern Inner Circle: Stone 106 in the foreground, with Stones 101-5 behind

largest at Avebury, over 7 m (23 ft) long and weighing over 20 tonnes.

Until Keiller's work of restoration in the 1930s, the Cove was shrouded with cottages and an unsightly garage that clustered close to it. These have now been demolished, but the old banks and field boundaries can still be seen. Much of the interior of the Avebury circle was covered in cottages and sheds, gardens and orchards.

Around the outer edge of the North-east Sector, a substantial ridge can be seen. These were walls delimiting the fields of the interior. The berm on the inside slope of the bank is particularly clear. This was presumably designed to stop excess soil slippage from the bank into the ditch when first constructed.

The **South-east Sector** was partly excavated and restored by Keiller in 1939. Before that, Gray had investigated the ditch near the southern causeway. Keiller's work concentrated on the area of the Southern Circle, where Stukeley had recorded the great Obelisk at its centre. 'The central obelisk of this temple is of circular form at base, of a vast bulk, 21 ft long and 8 ft 9 in in diameter; when standing, higher than the rest'. Stukeley recorded the Obelisk in its fallen position in 1723. It was smashed up for building stone some years later. Four pits were recorded behind the Obelisk, and these are now marked by round concrete markers. In the last century maypoles were erected in the area of the Obelisk.

Stone 98, one of the two huge Portal Stones that guard the southern entrance of Avebury Circle

South-west Sector: Stones 12-4, with Portal Stones and Southern Inner Circle behind

On one occasion, the digging opened up a pit behind the Obelisk and disclosed a prehistoric pot. Keiller's 1939 excavations revealed the north–south alignments of 12 stones called the Z-feature, which may have been intended as a symbolic enclosure around the Obelisk and its associated pits. Because of the outbreak of the Second World War in 1939, the excavations were terminated, and the eastern side of the Z-feature still remains unexplored. The stones of the southern circle were very substantial, and five are now visible. The original 29 stones were set up in a perfect circle, with an average of 11 m (36 ft) between each.

The Ring Stone stands to the southeast of the southern circle, and is visible now only as a broken stump. It was standing in 1724 when Stukelcy wrote 'an odd stone standing, not of great bulk. It has a hole wrought in it . . .' From more recent archaeological work, it has been shown that the original stone was replaced by a sarsen with a natural hole

South-west Sector: the Barber-Surgeon Stone (9), under which was discovered in 1938 the crushed skeleton of a medieval barber-surgeon. See photograph on page 49

through it. The packing around the stone was tabular lower chalk, from the base of the great ditch, thus dating that stone to after the building of the henge ditch. Blocking the southern causeway, the great Portal Stones 1 (4.1 m/13 ft 7 in high) and 98 (4.3 m/14 ft 2 in high) form an impressive entrance.

The **South-west Sector** is the most complete and spectacular following Keiller's restoration. Only the perimeter stones were investigated, but these produced important information. In particular, the discovery of the skeleton of a medieval barber-surgeon, under stone 9, provided dating evidence for the burial of many of the Avebury stones. The barber had accidentally been crushed by the stone as it fell into a purpose-dug pit at its base. He had in a small pouch at his waist, a pair of scissors, an iron probe

South-west Sector: Stones 8 and 9

and some coins that dated to c1310-20. The instruments suggest that he may have been an itinerant tradesman. Following his first tragedy in the fourteenth century, the barber seemed doomed, as his skeletal remains received a direct hit from a German bomb in the Second World War whilst being studied in London.

The last stone (no 24, near the High Street) was originally buried in the foundations of the blacksmith's forge. Its battered shape was partly restored by Keiller, from the broken fragments around it.

West Kennet Avenue

From the southern causeway entrance, the West Kennet Avenue follows a winding course over 2.3 km (1.5 miles), linking the Avebury Circles with the Sanctuary (see page 32).

South-west Sector: Stone 12. Sarsens were chosen for their shapes

South-west Sector: Stone 14

Tour

Leave the Circle from the southern entrance through the gates (see plan), cross the road and enter the Avenue field. The first third of the Avenue has been excavated and restored, and many of the original stones can be seen. Stone 19, the last one before the Avenue crosses the road, has some interesting axe-sharpening marks. The next portion of the Avenue now lies buried beneath cornfields. The southern portion of the Avenue has been badly damaged by the A4 road widening, and there is little to be seen today.

The National Trust is working towards a route which will allow you to walk the line of the Avenue up to the Sanctuary.

History

Aubrey and Stukeley both recorded the Avenue in the seventeenth and eighteenth centuries, and their records provided the incentive for Keiller's work on the site in

West Kennet Avenue from the air, looking south-east, with Avebury at base of the photo-graph (University of Cambridge collection)

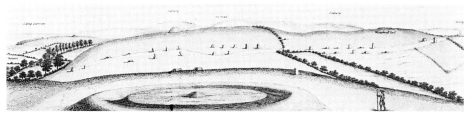

William Stukeley's view of the West Kennet Avenue in 1724

1934 and 1935. Like the stones of the Circle, the Avenue stones were buried in the medieval period and dragged away for building material in more recent times. In the last century, the Road Commissioners removed several of the stones that stood along the course of the A4 Bath road.

Description

Originally consisting of about 100 pairs of stones, the Avenue followed a sinuous course. The stones were about 15 m (49 ft) apart and there was a span of about 24 m (80 ft) between the pairs. Several had been buried in medieval times, and others had been removed altogether. Of those remaining none were very large, between cl.5 m (5 ft) and 3 m (10 ft) high. When Keiller began work,

only four stones were standing and a further nine were partly visible. Halfway down the Avenue, a curious Later Neolithic 'occupation' site came to light, producing a quantity of grooved ware pottery and fine flint tools. This may have been a special structure incorporated within the Avenue, or an earlier settlement. The winding course of the Avenue is curious; indeed, it may have avoided contemporary structures or settlement.

The dating of the Avenue is probably slightly later than the main henge and circles, probably c 2300BC, although no absolute dating is yet available. Material from the 'habitation' site was Late Neolithic (c 2500BC) Grooved and Peterborough types. At the foot of four of the excavated stones, Beaker period burials

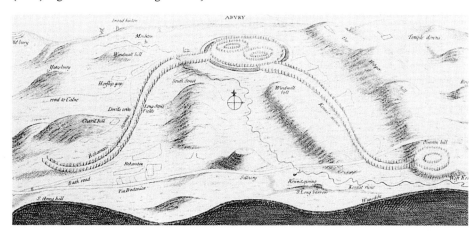

William Stukeley's dramatic map of Avebury and its avenues in 1743

Transporting a sarsen stone on rollers: an artist's impression

were found, accompanied with their distinctive pots. These may have been later than the erection of the stones. Rough estimates therefore put the building of the Avenue at *c* 2300-2100BC.

Beckhampton Avenue

Although recorded by William Stukeley in the eighteenth century, little remains visible today of the western avenue that may once have linked Avebury with other stones and circles. Stukeley drew two stones which stood in the High Street, and constructed the possible line of stones towards the still surviving Long Stones, or Adam and Eve (OS Ref SU 089693), situated north of the A4361, leading from Avebury to the Beckhampton roundabout. It is possible that the Long Stones were part of a separate circle or cove, with its own avenue, although recent excavations in gardens and modern pipelines have located the positions of some large sarsen stones that may be part of the lost Avenue.

Transportation and Erection of the Avebury Stones

The sarsen stones that were used in the building of the Avebury monuments were collected locally from the downland surrounding Avebury. The very size of the stones is impressive, since many weighed more than 20 tonnes, and some were over 60 tonnes. None of the stones have been worked, unlike Stonehenge where they had been shaped with stone mauls (hammers). However the stones have traces of ancient solution hollows, tree-root holes and rivulets made during the Oligocene and Miocene geological periods (between 30 and 20 million years ago) when the sarsen 'sandstone' was laid down as a layer over the cretaceous chalk of the Wiltshire Downs. Following chemical changes, the stone is now too hard for carving or shaping easily.

From experiments carried out with similar stones, the Avebury stones were probably dragged to Avebury from the surrounding downland and valleys on

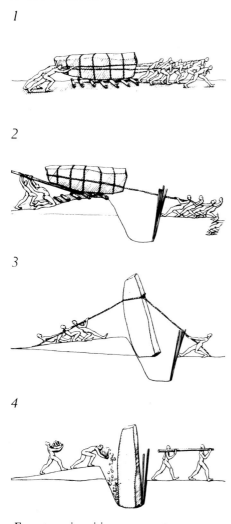

1

2

3

4

Four stages in raising a sarsen stone

Once the stones had been dragged to the selected positions, they were raised upright with simple wood levers and propped up in fairly shallow holes. Traces of smaller wooden posts were found behind the stones, which probably prevented the stone shifting as it was pulled upright. Packing stones were then forced around the base to prevent any further movement. Over the centuries, several inches of the chalk surface may have dissolved, making the stone holes shallower, and thus allowing the stones to fall.

Silbury Hill
(OS Ref SU 100686)

Tour
Visitors can walk from Avebury or drive by road. If walking, leave the main car park on the south side of Avebury, cross the A4361 and take the footpath following the stream south towards Silbury. After half a mile, cross the stream at the bridge, and continue along the footpath until you arrive at the Silbury car park and viewing area. Alternatively, drive via the A4 to the Silbury car park, and proceed to the viewing area.

Because Silbury Hill has been designated a Site of Special Scientific Interest, it is not possible to climb the hill, since this would damage the unique downland flora. Please help to protect the site.

History
Silbury Hill is the largest man-made mound in Europe, and is much the same size as some of the smaller pyramids of Egypt, and higher than the Mississippian mounds at Cahokia. It stands 39.5 m (130 ft high), and still remains, after two centuries of investigation, one of the most enigmatic of British prehistoric sites. Radiocarbon dating suggests the first

wooden rollers with leather ropes. Particular shapes seem to have been selected, either tall and column-shaped, or triangular. Certainly the stones surviving in the Avenue seem to have alternated between the two. Alexander Keiller suggested that they may have represented male (column) and female (triangular or lozenge) shapes.

William Stukeley's drawing of Silbury Hill and the Bath Road in 1723

Silbury Hill, photographed by Skyscan for English Heritage

phase dates from *c* 2660BC, and corresponds with the Later Neolithic period.

Recorded by both Aubrey and Stukeley, the hill was first investigated in 1776 by the Duke of Northumberland and Colonel Drax, who used a team of Cornish tin miners to sink a shaft from the top of the mound to the ground surface. Later, in 1849 the Archaeological Institute excavated an elaborate tunnel, 1 m (3 ft) wide and over 2 m (6 ft) high, directed by the engineer Henry Blandford and Dean Mereweather of Hereford. They burrowed through 30 m (100 ft) of solid chalk before encountering buried soils. They were expecting to find a burial chamber at the centre of the mound, but did not find any signs of one. Later, the Wiltshire Archaeological Society excavated under the eastern side of the mound in 1867 to see whether the Roman road (A4) went under the mound, and thus pre-dated the hill. They found the Roman road had been lined up on Silbury, but veered round it, showing conclusively that the hill was older than the Roman occupation of Britain. Further work in 1886 directed attention to the surrounding ditch of Silbury, and 10 pits were sunk into the ditch fill. The water table was reached at 2.5 m (8 ft), but probing suggested the ditch to be 5-6 m (16-20 ft) deep.

In 1922, the famous Egyptologist Sir Flinders Petrie excavated at the base of the mound, in search of a buried entrance to the suspected burial chamber that all antiquarians had believed lay at the centre of the mound. He too was frustrated, as only horizontal layers of chalk rubble were found. However, the 1849 tunnel still remained open and he explored the length of it, before it was sealed.

The original function of the hill remains a mystery, and this has encouraged much speculation as to its original purpose. Ideas have included romantic interpretations of mother goddesses, ley lines and unlikely astro-archaeological theories.

However, the most recent (1968-69) and most scientific excavations have provided a whole new and unsuspected range of information about Silbury Hill. Under the direction of Professor Richard Atkinson, with the BBC and Cardiff University, the project tunnelled to the centre of the hill, through all the layers that make up the present structure. Following a line close to the original 1849 tunnel, the new tunnel passed through what were three hitherto unsuspected phases of building at Silbury.

Silbury 1 At the centre of the mound, which lies on a small terrace projecting into the valley, a small mound was built from layers of muddy gravel from the valley and dark layers of turf and soil. The turf contained rich evidence of the insect life and flora that lived around Silbury some 2800 years BC. In particular, the ants preserved in the turf had just produced their summer flight wings, showing that the turf had been cut and placed in the mound in late July or August, perhaps following the completion of the harvest. The turf layer was held in place with a fence of wooden stakes. Over this were four layers of soil. The flora preserved gave a clear picture of the Neolithic downland environment. In all, this first phase of Silbury covered an area 37 m (120 ft) in diameter, and was 5 m (18 ft) high.

Silbury 2 Soon after the Silbury 1 structure was completed, Silbury 2, a larger mound, was built over it. This involved the partial digging of a deep surrounding ditch, 14 m (40 ft) wide and 7 m (20 ft) deep, enclosing an area of 110 m (350 ft) in diameter. Silbury 2 was formed of chalk rubble dug from the ditch, arranged in a complex series of reinforced walls shaped as a conical pyramid. The hill was 17 m (50ft) high. In all, about 28,325 cubic metres (1 million cubic feet) of chalk and soil were incorporated into the structure. Before Phase 2 Silbury was completed, there was a change of plan, and an even larger Silbury, Phase 3, was constructed over it.

Silbury 3 The third phase involved the filling in of the first ditch and the construction of a larger one, enclosing a further 1 ha (2.5 acres). The ditch was 7 m (20 ft) deep, and involved the transport of a further 184,136 cubic metres (6.5 million cubic feet) of chalk and soil in the building of the mound. As in Silbury 2, a precise method of chalk construction, with six horizontal steps of chalk to maintain the slope of the pyramid-like structure, was employed. When excavated, the chalk walls making up the individual steps (each 4.5-5 m/15-17 ft high) were formed of an intricate web of reinforcement walls, with the outer walls of each step built in large blocks of hard

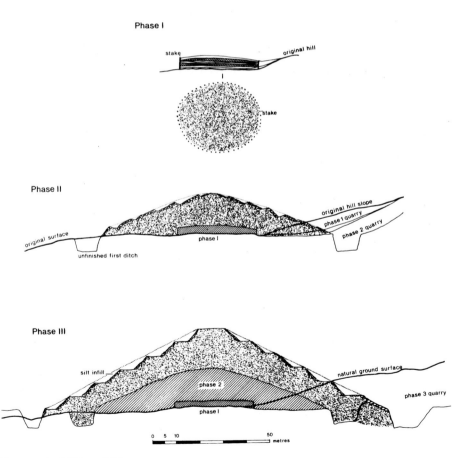

Phases 1–3 of Silbury Hill

lower chalk, reaching the total height of
39.5 m (130 ft). The outer walls leant in
at a steady 60-degree angle, thus making
the structure very stable. The prehistoric
builders had a good understanding of
basic soil mechanics, and Silbury was
unique for its advanced design. The steps
were then filled in with silt brought from
the huge quarry area that surrounds the
hill on the north and west sides. Only the
top step was not filled, and this can
clearly be seen today.

The hill covers an area of 2.2ha (5.5
acres). Of the total 350,000 cubic metres
(12.5 million cubic feet) of chalk and soil
that make up Silbury, 250,000 cubic
metres (8.75 million cubic feet) were
quarried with simple stone, bone, antler
and wooden tools, and transported in
wicker baskets. Only the bottom 9 m
(30 ft) of the hill are made up of the
natural terrace. The rest is entirely man-
made.

The hill represents one of the feats of
prehistoric construction, and its massive
size and obviously well-planned structure
suggest a high degree of social organisation, with perhaps, a small group of in-
fluential individuals, able to control a
very large workforce needed to build
Silbury. It has been calculated that 18
million man-hours went into building the
hill; that is to say, 700 men for 10 years.
Thus Silbury represents one of the most
labour-intensive sites in prehistoric
Europe.

Yet what was it intended for? We still
have few clues on how it was used or
why it was built. The location of Silbury
in the valley bottom is curious, since it
can be seen only from comparatively
nearby. When considered as part of the
massive Neolithic ceremonial complex of
Avebury, Silbury can be perceived as
part of a special man-made landscape in
the upper Kennett valley, its huge and
apparently useless structure perhaps

intended as a cenotaph or tribal marker.

Silbury Hill is not quite unique, since
about 5 miles to the east, again beside the
Kennett stream, is another, smaller but
similar Neolithic structure. This is the
much ruined Marlborough Mound,
which is located inside the grounds of
Marlborough College. Since neither hill
has produced any evidence for its original
function, we must speculate that the
structure itself may have been the important aspect, not what the hill contained.

In later times, Silbury was used by
both the Romans and Saxons for possible
burial, as a Roman surveying point, and
for a Saxon lookout and stronghold.
Related material has been found dug into
the surface of the mound.

Legends about Silbury abound, some
plausible and others less so. The most
well-known is that the hill contained the
burial of legendary King Sel. John
Aubrey wrote 'No history gives us any
account of this hill. The tradition only is
that King Sil (or Zel as the country folk
pronounce it) was buried here on horse-
back and that the hill was raised while a
posset of milk was seething'. By the
eighteenth century the legend had grown
and the King and his horse had become
life-size figures in solid gold.

West Kennet Long Barrow
(OS Ref SU 105677)

Tour

The barrow is located a third of a mile
south of the A4, and is reached by
footpath. Either proceed on foot from the
Silbury Hill viewing area, east along the
A4 for a quarter of a mile to the lay-by
beside the footpath; or park your car
in the lay-by. Proceed across the water-
meadow, over the stream, and along the
footpath to the barrow on the hill crest.

West Kennet Long Barrow from the east, with the entrance in the foreground

It is possible to enter the chambers of the barrow, and from the top of the mound there are good views of Silbury, the East Kennet Barrow, the Sanctuary and Windmill Hill.

History

The West Kennet Long Barrow is one of the largest and best-preserved Neolithic burial chambers in Britain. It was recorded by John Aubrey, who included a sketch in his unpublished *Monumenta Britannica* of *c*1665, and described it 'on the brow of the Hill, south of West Kynnet, is this monument, but without any name. It is about the length of the former [a barrow near Marlborough]; but at the end, only rude greyweather-stones tumbled together; the barrow is about half a yard high'. William Stukeley made more accurate drawings of the barrow between 1720-24, showing the ditch and the stones. Both Aubrey and Stukeley recorded that the barrow was regularly dug into by a local doctor, probably to supply bones for potions and medicines. Stukeley wrote 'Dr Took as they call him, has miserably defaced the South Long Barrow by digging half the length of it. It was most neatly smoothed out to a sharp ridge'. Dr Toope wrote to Aubrey in 1685 telling him of his discoveries at the nearby Sanctuary, where he had found workmen digging up human bones. He wrote 'I quickly perceived that they were humane, and came next day and dugg for them, and stored myselfe with many bushells, of which I made a noble medicine that relieved many of my distressed neighbours.'

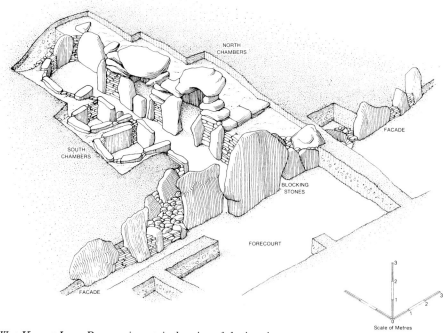

West Kennet Long Barrow: isometric drawing of the interior

Aubrey noted that 'Dr Toope was lately at the Golgatha again to supply a defect of medicine he had from hence'. At the barrow, much of the disturbance found by the 1955 excavations in the forecourt was probably caused by Toope's diggings. Stukeley called it the 'Archdruid's barrow' and described it as standing 'east to west, pointing to the dragon's head on Overton Hill [the] huge stones piled one upon the other ... doubtless in order to form a sufficient chamber for the remains of the person there buried'.

In 1859, Dr Thurnam excavated the central passage and end-chamber of the barrow in his search for skeletal material of the Ancient British (*Crania Britannica*, 1865). In 1882, the barrow, together with Silbury Hill, came under the protection of the first Ancient Monuments Act, and this finally stopped the damage done by local people digging for chalk or cutting turf from the mound.

The barrow was most recently excavated by Piggott and Atkinson in 1955 - 56. Thurnam's report of the single passage and chamber was inconsistent with evidence from other barrows, which had chambers off the main passage. The 1955–56 work revealed that, indeed, four small chambers, two on either side, were preserved as they had been left in the late Neolithic, 4000 years ago.

Structure

The West Kennet Barrow has traditionally been seen as a blend of two separate burial traditions. The stone-built passage and chambers are related to Neolithic

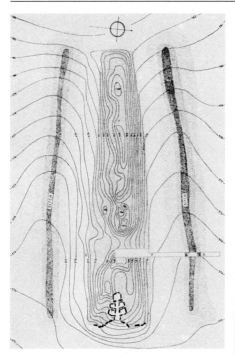

Contoured plan of the West Kennet Long Barrow, showing the lateral ditches

the rest being made up of sarsen boulders, and chalk, excavated from two parallel ditches either side of the trapezoidal mound. The now silted ditches are some 10 m (33 ft) outside the mound, and were originally 3–4 m (12 ft) deep. From the findings at more recently excavated barrows, it is likely that the earthen part of the barrow may have contained wooden or hurdle divisions providing areas for burial. The bulk of the earthen mound has not yet been investigated.

The stone passage and chambers are constructed chiefly of local sarsen stones that provided uprights or orthostats for the walls, and flat capstones for the roofs of the chambers. Smaller sarsens and specially imported oolitic limestone slabs from the Bath-Frome and Caine areas, to the west, were used to infill the gaps in the walls, and provide the corbelling for the capstones. Originally, when the tomb was in use, the entrance would have been a curved forecourt, perhaps for funerary ceremonies. Once the tomb was filled, the Beaker people closed the entrance by filling the chambers, passage and forecourt with earth and stones, and blocked the entrance with the three huge upright stones that block it today. The blocking seems to have been an important and

chambered tombs in the west and north of Britain, and the earthen long barrow is typical of the Earlier Neolithic in lowland Britain. The barrow is related to a group known as the Severn-Cotswold type, that are scattered west from Wiltshire to South Wales. Other barrows of this group include Wayland's Smithy, Hetty Pegler's Tump, Stoney Littleton, Adam's Grave and the nearby East Kennet long barrow. Recent radiocarbon dates now indicate that these tombs were in use from as early as 3700–3500BC and continued until the Beaker people of the late third millennium BC around 2000BC.

The structure is huge, and second only to East Kennet Barrow, is the longest in Britain, 100 m (328 ft) in length. The stone chambers extend only *c*12 m (40 ft),

Burials in the north-east chamber, as excavated by Piggott in 1955–56

West Kennet Long Barrow. An artist's impression of a burial taking place. In the foreground are the huge slabs which finally blocked and sealed the entrance

final gesture to the use of ancestral tombs, which ceased to be used after c2200-2000BC.

Inside the passage, on the south side, one of the large upright stones shows signs of having been used as a polishing stone, probably before it was incorporated into the tomb. The polished axes of the Neolithic had to be ground into shape on rough sandstone, and the local sarsen provided an ideal material.

Burials

In all, the skeletal parts of some 46 individuals had been buried on the floor of the barrow, over a period of at least 1500 years, from the first construction of the barrow, c3700BC, until the Beaker period in the late Neolithic c2000BC. Few of the individuals were articulated (only one was complete), and mostly bones had been jumbled up with the successive opening and insertion of new bodies into the tomb. Some bones had been tidied into heaps, with a row of skulls in the southwest chamber, and heaps of vertebrae and long bones. The final Beaker-period burial placed in the north-east chamber of the tomb, before it was closed, was the complete skeleton of an elderly man. The body was in a crouched position. As well as having a fractured arm, an abscess on one shoulder and deformed toes, he had apparently died from an arrowhead embedded in the throat.

Analysis of the skeletal material from the tomb was interesting, since nearly all the adults had arthritis, and some showed signs of *spina bifida*. There were several children, and recent researches suggest that the four side chambers and the large end chamber were used for the different age and sex groups of the community that used the barrow. Thus, the west chamber was predominantly used for adult males, the north-east and west

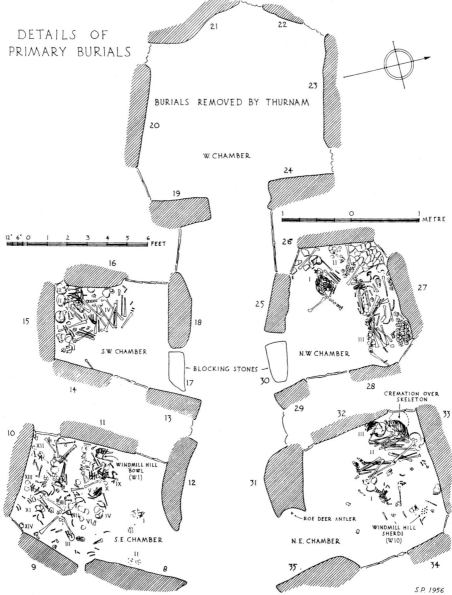

DETAILS OF PRIMARY BURIALS

BURIALS REMOVED BY THURNAM

W. CHAMBER

S.W. CHAMBER

N.W. CHAMBER

BLOCKING STONES

S.E. CHAMBER

WINDMILL HILL BOWL (W1)

N.E. CHAMBER

CREMATION OVER SKELETON

ROE DEER ANTLER

WINDMILL HILL SHERDS (W10)

METRE

FEET

S.P. 1956

West Kennet Long Barrow: details of the burial deposits excavated in 1955–56

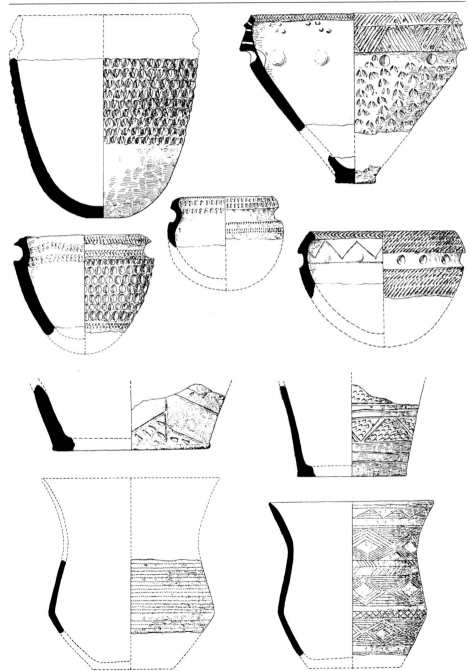

West Kennet Long Barrow: examples of pottery from the Earlier to Late Neolithic

chambers for mixed adults, the south-east for the old and the south-west chamber for children.

The discrepancy between the numbers of skulls and long bones and the actual number of individuals buried in the tomb suggests that only some parts of the skeleton were selected for burial, or remained long in the tomb. Certainly, the number of fragmentary human skulls and long bones from the contemporary ditches of Windmill Hill could be interpreted in terms of the ritual use of some bones at the camp, following removal of them from the barrow. The fragmentary nature of some of the skeletons also suggests that many of the burials were interred long after the flesh had rotted from the bones, and only the dry, sometimes scorched, bones were placed in the barrow. The large quantity of skeletal material from the Sanctuary (see page 35) suggests that the circular buildings may have been some type of mortuary house, where bodies were perhaps allowed to rot, before the burial of some bones in the barrows.

It is possible that the long barrow, of which there are several around the parish of Avebury, served clans or extended families. The tombs may have been regarded as the place of the ancestors, and thus demonstrated in monumental scale the continuity of one generation to the next and their link to the local area. Some of the long barrows, such as South Street and Beckhampton Road, seem to have contained no human remains at all, and may have instead been symbolic cenotaphs.

Grave goods

The pottery from the barrow covered a long range of time, from the Earlier to Late Neolithic: Windmill Hill plain bowls, Peterborough decorated Middle Neolithic types (Mortlake, Fengate and Ebbsfleet), Rinyo-Clacton Grooved Wares, as well as the later Long-necked, Bell and Corded Beakers. In all, fragments of some 250 different vessels were found. Other grave goods included bone, stone and shell beads, flint tools and animal bones.

Following the 1955–56 excavation, the stone chambers were restored, and the capstones and fallen façade stones re-erected by the Ministry of Works.

The Sanctuary
(OS Ref SU 118679)

Tour

The Sanctuary is located on the south side of the A4 on Overton Hill, at the junction of the Ridgeway Long Distance Footpath, half a mile east of Silbury Hill. It may be reached by car or by walking along the Avenue (page 17). The circular buildings of the Sanctuary are now marked by concrete posts, which show the different phases of building.

From the Sanctuary, several very impressive Bronze Age round barrows can be seen, on the north side of the A4, at the beginning of the Ridgeway path. The line of the Roman road is also visible as a slight ridge on the east side of the Ridgeway. Almost opposite the Roman road, on the west side of the Ridgeway, another stone circle was recorded, although nothing can be detected today. There are fine views towards the West Kennet Long Barrow to the south-west, the East Kennet Long Barrow on the southern horizon (now covered by beech trees), and the reconstructed part of the West Kennet Avenue to the north-west and Silbury Hill to the west.

History

Recorded by Aubrey and Stukeley, the

The Sanctuary, photographed by Skyscan for English Heritage

stones of the Sanctuary and its connection with the West Kennet Avenue were intact until destroyed in 1724. Aubrey described the Sanctuary briefly and inaccurately: 'on the brow of the hill, is another monument, encompassed with a circular trench, and a double circle of stones, four or five feet high, tho most are now fallen down' (1648). Samuel Pepys also recorded seeing the Sanctuary in his Diary in 1668, 'so took coach again, seeing one place with great high stones pitched round, which, I believe, was once some particular building, in some measure like that of Stonehenge'. More than half a century later, Stukeley recorded much about the Sanctuary and witnessed its destruction by a local

builder, Tom Robinson, who cleared the ground in 1724 'to gain a little dirty profit'. Stukeley considered the Sanctuary to be the terminus or 'head' of the 'great Serpent', that was represented by the two avenues of Avebury, and this theory became hopelessly entangled with his later ideas of druids at Avebury.

No excavation took place at the Sanctuary during the nineteenth century, when the location was forgotten. It was not until 1930 that Maud Cunnington, inspired by the excavation at Woodhenge near Stonehenge, decided to relocate the site. Unfortunately the site was dug in a piecemeal fashion and little attention was paid to anything but the position of the plentiful post and stone-holes. In fact,

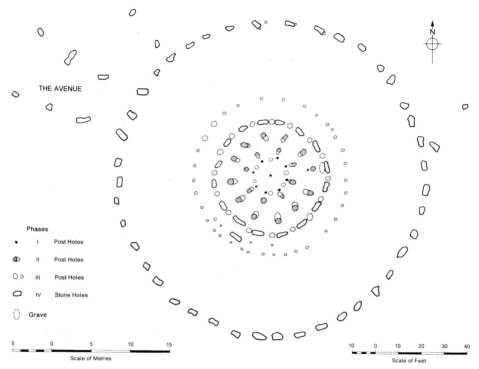

Plan of the Sanctuary, showing Phases 1–4

the Sanctuary was shown to be a multi-phase structure of three or four successive circular buildings.

Description

The first building at the Sanctuary was constructed *c*3000BC, a small circular wooden hut consisting of eight outer posts and a central post. It was about 4.5 m (15 ft) in diameter. Presumably, this small structure marked an important spot, because the original hut, Phase 1, was later surrounded by a larger, and more complex building, Phase 2. The second building was more than twice as large, just over 10 m (33 ft) in diameter, with twelve large upright posts supporting the outer wall, and eight more posts supporting the inner roof edge. It is presumed that the centre of the circular building was open to the sky.

The Third Phase was still larger and was built possibly several hundred years after Phases 1 and 2. This structure consisted of wooden posts in three concentric rings. Some 20 m (65 ft) in diameter, the building may have had an elaborate entrance on the south-west side. Finally, in Phase 4, standing stones were incorporated with the Phase 3 building, so that two concentric rings of stone, one set between the second circle of posts, and the other about 12 m (40 ft) outside the building, surrounded the original structure. The outer stone circle had its entrance marked by three larger stones, opening into the West Kennet Avenue on the north-west side, and this 'entrance' marked the beginning of the ceremonial routeway.

Under the most eastern stone of the inner stone circle, the burial of a young man accompanied by a beaker was found. It may have been a dedication burial, or even sacrifice, placed inside the circle sometime about 2300-2000BC.

Pottery of Windmill Hill, Peterborough, and Beaker types was found together with a number of quite fine flint tools. There was also a considerable quantity of human bone.

The function of the Sanctuary is unclear, but it is similar to several other circular wooden buildings both near and within henge sites. Within the henge at Durrington Walls, near Stonehenge, two such buildings were excavated, and several others located. The classic building at Woodhenge, apart from its outer ditch, is comparable with the Sanctuary. The henges of Marden and Mount Pleasant also produced traces of circular structures. There may even have been circular wooden buildings within

PHASE I

PHASE II

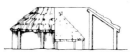

PHASE III & IV

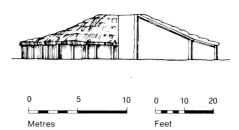

The Sanctuary: elevations of Phases 1-4, based on the evidence of post-holes

Avebury, before the stone circles were erected. The location of such buildings in the henges, or at the termini of avenues connected with henges must be significant. It is likely that they were used for ritual and ceremonial purposes, perhaps associated with burial cults, worship and feasts.

Windmill Hill
(OS Ref SU 086715)

Tour
Windmill Hill can be reached either by car or on foot.

By car leave Avebury on the A4361, heading towards Beckhampton, Devizes and Bath. After a quarter of a mile, turn

The Sanctuary: an artist's impression of how it might have appeared during its final phase, viewed from the Avenue

right, taking the road to Avebury Trusloe
and Windmill Hill. Pass the houses and
follow the signs, left, to Windmill Hill for
half a mile. Very limited parking space is
available. Do not try to take a car any
further.

On foot from Avebury, leave from the
bottom of the High Street, and follow the
footpath, over the river and bear right
past Trusloe Manor. The path enters
Bray Street, which leads to a paved track
heading to Windmill Hill. The distance is
about one and a quarter miles from
Avebury.

Passing the parking area, follow the
track up the hill on foot to the kissing-
gate. Enter Windmill Hill and proceed
slightly to the left of the barrows. The
banks and ditches are just detectable on
the south-west side of the hill, and are
more visible on the east, where excavation cleared them of silt. The numerous
Bronze Age barrows are well-preserved
examples, dating from c1500BC. Either
return the same way, or take the path
from the stile on the south-east side of
the hill. Follow the fence east, and before
crossing the stream, follow the path on
the right across the field, until reaching
the paved footpath. Then retrace steps to
Avebury village.

History
Windmill Hill is regarded as the classic
Neolithic causewayed 'camp' or enclosure
in southern Britain, since it was the first
to be excavated and the finds from it
have been regarded as typical of the
Earlier to Middle Neolithic. The site first
came to notice in the early years of this
century, when plentiful scatters of flint
and pottery were picked up by the vicar
of Winterbourne Monkton, the Rev
Kendall. During the early 1920s, O G S
Crawford, archaeologist of the Ordnance
Survey, became aware of plans to build a
Marconi wireless station on the hill. He

notified his colleague, Alexander Keiller.
Keiller was an interested amateur archaeologist and the wealthy heir of the marm-
alade fortunes of Dundee. He suggested
that efforts be made to buy the site, and
thus save one of the very few known
Neolithic open sites from destruction.
Keiller bought the site himself in 1924–
25, and began excavations, first under the
direction of H St George Gray, and then
by himself. Excavations continued for
five years, and these were pioneering in
archaeological methodology and the use
of modern equipment. Two distinct
phases were identified, an Earlier Neolithic pre-enclosure settlement of
c3700BC, and the Middle Neolithic causewayed camp. Later, sporadic occupation
during the Beaker period left traces of
pottery in the upper levels of the ditches.
Further excavations were conducted
by Isobel Smith in 1957-58, in order to
clarify the sequence of the ditches and
obtain dating and environmental samples.

Description
Windmill Hill is a low hill (600 ft above
sea level), 1 mile north-west of Avebury.
Three rings of concentric ditches enclose
the largest Neolithic causewayed enclosure known, 8.5 ha (21 acres). The
ditches are non-continuous, interrupted
by small chalk causeways between each
section. The outer ditch was deepest
2.1 m (7 ft), the middle ditch 1.4 m (4 ft 7
in), and the inner ditch 0.95 m (3 ft 1 in).
Three rings of banks on the inside
edge of the ditches originally enclosed the
site, and it was probably to obtain the
chalk rubble for the banks that the ditches
were dug. The excavation was
done with simple antler picks and rakes,
ox shoulder-blade shovels, and wooden or
stone tools. Each short stretch was
probably dug by small gangs of people,
and their labour amounted to some 62-
64,000 man-hours of work, probably over

Windmill Hill causewayed enclosure, photographed in 1949 (University of Cambridge)

many years, perhaps for a short season each year. The banks may have been revetted with timber, or have had some type of fencing along the top.

Although few traces have been found of substantial structures within the enclosure, it is likely that flimsy buildings were erected for the seasonal activities that took place. There is some evidence of a more substantial rectangular building under the inner bank, near the centre of the enclosure, that might have pre-dated the banks and ditches. Just outside the outer bank on the eastern side, a square enclosure, measuring 8.8 m x 9.1 m (29 ft x 30 ft) was found (between two round barrows), and this, although not precisely dated, appears to have been a timber building, with large posts set in a shallow trench. Twelve posts were also set inside the ditches, and may have been from an earlier structure. Although there was little material found in the structure, the presence of 'foreign' oolitic limestone, as found in the West Kennet Long Barrow, and some bone, suggests a parallel possible mortuary use. The palisade is comparable with the barrow excavated at Fussell's Lodge near Salisbury (SU 191324 on private land), and a possible interpretation is that the square enclosure was used for exposing human remains before final burial. It might also have had a utilitarian use, such as a cattle pen.

Neolithic life on Windmill Hill

The excavations at Windmill Hill were

Plan of Windmill Hill

important for revealing the first clear picture of Earlier Neolithic life in southern Britain, although the data from the site were not from a permanent settlement. Ecological data showed that the area was wooded with hazel, blackthorn, hawthorn, oak and ash in a mixed woodland habitat. The economy was based on Emmer and Eincorn wheat and barley, supplemented with crab apples, flax (perhaps for thread), wild cherry and hazel nuts. Domestic cattle and sheep with some pigs were reared, and these appear to have been kept for meat, since the mature animals were butchered. Wild animals included red and roe deer, and wild pig and cattle, and hares and birds were snared and hunted. Fox and wild cat were caught, probably for their decorative furs, and dogs were kept for

Windmill Hill: an artist's impression of a burial ceremony at the square enclosure, which may have been a mortuary (see page 37). The causewayed ditches are visible beyond

hunting and herding.

Activities on Windmill Hill may have been seasonal, since the butchery of animals appears to have taken place in the spring and autumn. At the short-term camps on the hill, people used pottery, had large fires, made flint tools, and ground flour on quern stones. Animals skins were processed for making leather garments, tents and thongs. Axes from stone sources far from Wiltshire were used to cut down trees and to shape timber for building. Less everyday activities included what appears to be ritual deposition of rubbish, animal bones and complete skeletons along the bottoms of the ditches. Human bodies both complete and in fragments were also buried in the ditches. The general picture is of a farming community, living in a prosperous

Windmill Hill vessels were generally roundbased. Some had lugs for suspending them

and relatively peaceful environment, occasionally interrupted with large social gatherings at the causewayed enclosure.

The phasing of the site falls into several periods, and it seems likely that, although not permanent, the enclosure was regularly in use. The first-phase use in c3700BC by Early Neolithic communities was pre-enclosure, and occupation was on the summit of the hill. The second phase, the Windmill Hill period, lasted from c3500 to 3000BC. During this phase, the three enclosures were dug, not necessarily at the same time, and the Square Enclosure was in use. The bulk of Neolithic material found at the site dates from this period. The third phase was represented by more sporadic use in the Later Neolithic, and Peterborough

and Beaker pottery was deposited in the ditches. Finally, during the Bronze Age, round barrows were constructed and there appears to have been no domestic use of the site. Roman material was found scattered over the tops of the ditches, and a Roman villa was located on the western slopes of the hill.

A second causewayed enclosure on Overton Hill, only 3 miles from Windmill Hill, has recently been discovered. Nowhere else have two enclosures been found so close together. It may be that the two sites were not contemporary, or, if they were, that they served different functions, or even different communities. The Overton Hill site has not yet been investigated and remains a mystery.

HISTORY

Neolithic Background

The monuments of Avebury all date from the Neolithic period between about 6000 and 4000 years ago. Long before the adoption of agricultural practices and domestic plants and animals, Avebury was intermittently visited by the nomadic Mesolithic people, who had exploited the area for hunting and fishing, during the period following the last glacial epoch, some 10,000–7,000 years ago.

The changes that led to the settled agricultural life-style of the Neolithic were varied and complex, but certain characteristics were typical. From the seasonal camps of the Mesolithic groups, the Neolithic communities settled in permanent villages. The hunting and gathering economies were replaced by farming, with domestic animals and cereals (cattle, sheep, pigs; wheat, barley, oats, peas and beans). The formerly wooded environment was gradually cleared and cultivated, and within a few generations the landscape of Britain was indelibly engraved with the mark of man. Fields, trackways, settlements and buildings, as well as the massive and impressive ceremonial monuments, soon became prominent features of the landscape. Within the space of 2–3,000 years, the Neolithic communities of Britain evolved an economy, social structure and landscape that formed the beginnings of the modern world.

Earlier Neolithic

The earliest Neolithic communities (c4000–3000BC) left few substantial traces

of their activities except in the form of burial monuments, the long barrows, and the ditched enclosures, known as the causewayed camps. At Avebury, the earliest traces of Neolithic activity have been found buried under the long barrows. At South Street Long Barrow, 1 mile to the west of Avebury, traces of Neolithic ploughing were detected in the buried soil, and were dated to c3600BC, some 200 years before the barrow was constructed. At about the same time, the first open settlement on Windmill Hill was in use. The environmental evidence from studies on fossil pollens suggests that the downland around Avebury was densely wooded, and that only small patches of ground were cleared and cultivated. By 3500BC, agriculture was probably well established and there may have been a related population increase, based on the predictable food supplies and relatively comfortable living conditions that Neolithic life provided.

Causewayed Enclosures
From about 3500BC hilltop sites located at the centre of fertile and densely populated areas became the focus of activity as 'causewayed enclosures'. Windmill Hill at Avebury, surrounded by a large Neolithic population, was enclosed with three concentric rings of banks and ditches, forming a prominent, if windy, place for communal activities. Recently a further causewayed enclosure has been identified on Overton Hill from aerial photographs.

There has been much debate over recent years on the function of the enclosures. There are now scores of causewayed enclosure sites known in Britain, but few have produced similar data, and

Neolithic tools, weapons and pottery

a single common function has not been identified. Some were clearly living places; others, such as Hambledon Hill in Dorset, seem to have been primarily used for burial activities. Windmill Hill has produced a wide range of evidence, suggesting that it was used seasonally, in the spring and autumn, for coralling and butchering animals. Perhaps animals were brought from a wide area for culling, exchanging and butchering. Other activities included the production of flint tools, particularly scrapers, which could have been used to prepare the hides of the freshly butchered animals. Combs made from antler may have been used to tease the hair from the skins. Pottery was used in quantity, and some types made in areas distant from Avebury were brought to the enclosure. Exotic stone axes, derived from sources in northern and western Britain as well as some rarer flint

tools, were also imported. All this evidence suggests that the site acted as the focus for widely spread communities, congregating at Windmill Hill for seasonal markets, feasting and other social activities. Few traces of any permanent buildings have been located at Windmill Hill, and it seems likely that simple tents and flimsy huts were used for the short periods of activity. At the same time, a more gruesome aspect is the presence of human bones, and even whole bodies, buried in the ditches surrounding the site. One complete skeleton of a man was recently discovered and another, a child of about three years, who had died from water on the brain, was excavated by Keiller in the 1920s. Skulls and long bones were particularly frequent, and this suggests that some type of ritual activity, requiring the bones of the ancestors, took place on the hill.

Chronology of the Avebury Monuments

All dates are approximate

Date (calendar years)	Avebury monuments	Landscape, culture, sites elsewhere
First Neolithic		
4300BC		First forest clearance and agriculture
3800BC	Cultivation (under Horslip Barrow)	Farming in Avebury area. Early plain pottery
Early Neolithic		
3700BC	Windmill Hill open settlement. West Kennet Long Barrow	Hamlets in valleys and on river terraces. First burials in barrows, marking territories
3600BC	Cultivation (under South Street Barrow)	Landscape becoming clearer Fields and settlements
3500BC	Knapp Hill causewayed enclosure	First co-operative monuments constructed
3400BC	South Street Long Barrow	
Middle Neolithic		
3300BC	Windmill Hill causewayed enclosure	Robin Hood's Ball causewayed enclosure
3200BC	Beckhampton Long Barrow	Stonehenge Phase 1
3000BC	The Sanctuary Phase 1 and Windmill Hill square enclosure	Decorated pottery. New flint tools
Later Neolithic		
2800BC		Landscape degeneration with scrub
2700BC	The Sanctuary Phase 2 Silbury Hill Phase 1	Stonehenge Cursus. Grooved pottery
2600BC	Windmill Hill use declines Avebury probably begun	
2500BC	Silbury Hill Phase 2. The Sanctuary Phase 3. Silbury Hill Phase 3	Woodhenge, Durrington Walls, Marden henge
Final Neolithic		
2400BC	Avebury stones probably erected. West Kennet and Beckhampton Avenues	Beaker pottery
2300BC	Avebury Circles, Avenues and Sanctuary completed	Long barrows cease to be used
2200BC	West Kennet Long Barrow sealed	Economic expansion, agricultural regeneration
Early Bronze Age		
2100BC	Beaker burials in Avebury and Avenue	Stonehenge 2 (Bluestones)
2100BC		Stonehenge 3a (Sarsen circle)
1900–1800BC	Round barrows	Wessex culture. Stonehenge 3b

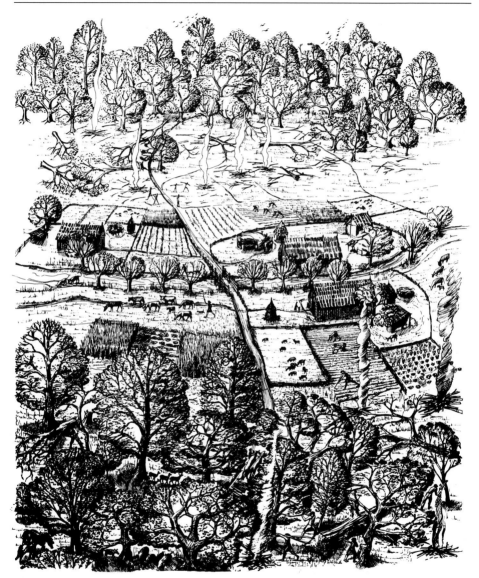

Artist's impression of the Neolithic landscape with forest clearance and early settlements

A number of 'ritual' pits were also found, filled with specially placed flints and stones. The banks of the camp may have had palisades of posts along their crest, and the sides may have been supported with hurdling. It seems unlikely that the camps were fortified, since there were numerous entrances. However, the enclosures may have had a symbolic function, demarcating the camps as special areas where ritual activities took place. Indeed, the function of the causewayed enclosures may have been similar to that of the henges that replaced them, their construction and use being devoted to economic, ceremonial and symbolic activities that would have played an important role in the life of simple agricultural communities.

The environmental reconstruction of the landscape of this Earlier Neolithic period suggests that most of the area was densely wooded with mixed deciduous forest. Initially, Windmill Hill may have been one of a few clearings in the area. The main domestic animal was probably pig, since it thrived in the woodlands. Sheep and cattle required open pasture, and may have been fewer. By the time the ditches were dug, much of the initial woodland had been replaced by fields and pasture, and there was a corresponding increase in cattle and sheep.

Long Barrows

The Long Barrows were in use throughout the Earlier Neolithic period, and continued to be used until the end of the Neolithic. They probably increased in number about 3000BC with the rise in population. Around Avebury there were a score of barrows within five miles, each one perhaps serving a clan or extended family. Different building traditions were incorporated into the barrows, some being composed only of soil, wood and chalk, others with chambers, constructed of sarsen and imported limestone. Grave goods were of simple, undecorated Windmill Hill type pottery, flint tools, and stone and bone beads. The siting of the barrows seems to have been important, with the crest of hills chosen so that the chalk mound would be seen from a considerable distance. Adam's Grave, 8 km (5 miles) to the south of Avebury, is a particularly prominent example, where lateral ditches were dug in order to emphasise the height of the barrow. Both

the East and West Kennet Barrows are visible from great distances, and in particular from the Kennet valley, along which Neolithic people doubtless travelled. Apart from providing a monument to their ancestors, the builders of the barrows may have given a clear signal to other communities that the clan using the barrow also laid claim to that particular territory. Other barrows such as South Street, to the west of Avebury, were less prominent and may have fulfilled an altogether different function.

Social structure

Understanding the social organisation of the Earlier Neolithic is difficult, since the traces are scanty. However, it seems probable that the Avebury area supported a fairly dense population. Agriculture was based on the fertile soils of the Kennet valley, with grazing on the slopes of the downland. The skeletal evidence from the long barrows suggests that families were buried in them. The area probably had several clans of extended families or segmentary lineages each with their own tomb, possibly their own small hamlet, but sharing the communal use of the causewayed camp. There is no evidence of chiefs, but the scanty number of burials in the tombs indicates that only some individuals were given a proper burial. What happened to the others we do not know. Grave goods were not especially rich and, from this, we must presume that in the Earlier Neolithic, material goods were not used to symbolise personal power or influence. Families may have been directed by the elder members, or by a particular clan group.

Later Neolithic

The Later Neolithic was very different

Early Bronze Age ornaments, pottery and weapons

from the earlier 'Windmill Hill' period. The environment changed from a fertile area to one which had been badly over-grazed. The woodland and small fields had been partially replaced by scrub and rough pasture, with small areas of cultivation. Bracken and thorn bushes may well have covered areas formerly farmed. At the same time, the population and its settlements had grown much denser in the Avebury area.

Along with the social and man-induced ecological changes, the economy had also changed. Animals were used for traction (ploughing), milk and wool, as well as meat. Agricultural practices had become more extensive, with the ploughing of formerly peripheral areas on the downs, grazing over the uplands, and the management of woodland areas.

The formerly undifferentiated, egalitarian society had become more structured and leaders, perhaps local tribal chiefs, had influence over considerable numbers of people. Warfare began to become a feature in a landscape already too full of rival groups, each needing more land and power. The burials in the long barrows now included complete corpses of individuals who may have died in battle, such as the last burial in the West Kennet barrow, who had an arrowhead embedded in the neck. All this suggests that life was not entirely peaceful.

The landscape was changed in other ways, with the building of the massive Later Neolithic monuments that characterise Avebury. From *c*2700 until 2000BC the entire landscape of Avebury was planned and changed. First, Silbury Hill was constructed. Soon after, the Sanctuary was enlarged. Then the great henge at Avebury was dug, and the stones put into position, and finally linked to the Sanctuary by the West Kennet Avenue. Other stone circles such as the Falkner Ring were constructed, and the Beckhampton Avenue may have connected another circle with Avebury. By the end of the third millenium (2000BC), long barrows were abandoned in favour of smaller round barrows with individual and small family burials. The emphasis had changed from a group identity to an individual one, yet with the great monuments to express the communal beliefs and activities.

The building of the great monuments is one of the most perplexing, yet fasci-nating, aspects of Later Neolithic Britain. A fantastic amount of labour was needed to construct Silbury and Avebury. The organisation of a workforce large enough to construct the monuments has prompted many theories about how such a society was governed. The current evidence for settlement in the Avebury area is scarce, but it has been suggested that a population of perhaps 10,000 people occupied the Marlborough Downs, and as many as 50,000 may have occupied Wessex. From that population, large, perhaps seasonal, gangs of workers, could have come to Avebury, after the harvest was completed, to construct the sites. But what encouraged them? Was it that they were forced to work as a tribute to a local leader? Or did religious beliefs necessitate that the great temple at Avebury and its associated structures had

Stratified layers of the Avebury Circle ditch excavated by H St George Gray, 1908–22

to be completed to appease now-forgotten gods? Whatever force stimulated the work, it is clear that the millions of man-hours of labour devoted to the Avebury monuments were the result of communal effort, directed towards monuments for communal activities.

Artefacts

The Later Neolithic brought new types of highly decorated pottery, new forms of flint tools and arrowheads, and the skill of weaving and spinning wool. Pottery falls into three phases during this period. First, the Peterborough types (Mortlake, Fengate and Ebbsfleet) from 3000 to 2300BC which had heavy decorated rims and geometric patterns incised into the surface. The later Grooved and Rinyo-Clacton type pottery (2500–1800BC) was also decorated, but with different styles of incised and embossed patterns. Finally, from c2300 to 1800BC, the Beakers, (bell, long-necked and corded types) became the chief type of pottery on both settlements and in graves. This was finely made, with intricate geometric patterns incised and impressed into the surface. All these pottery types have been found at Avebury, the Avenue, the Sanctuary and the West Kennet Barrow.

The leaf arrowheads of the Earlier Neolithic were gradually replaced by oblique tranchet and large barbed and tanged types. New flint tools included elaborate daggers and knives, ground stone maceheads, plaques and axes, and carved stone and chalk. By the Beaker period, metal was in use, with copper knives and hammered gold discs and jewellery.

These social, economic and technological changes provided the background for the emergence of the Bronze Age Wessex Culture of the second millenium BC, from c1800 to 1200BC. Although Avebury and its associated monuments may have been

in use during the earlier part of the Bronze Age, the most prominent features of the period are the many round barrows on Windmill Hill, Overton Hill and along the Ridgeway. Rich and rare artefacts, pottery, bronze and amber were the grave goods in these tombs. The round barrows were the tombs of a few prominent and perhaps wealthy individuals, in a society that had become very much more structured and hierarchial than the simple, egalitarian Neolithic society that first tamed the landscape of Avebury.

Later History

During the Late Bronze Age and Iron Age, from 1200BC to AD100, there seems to have been little activity around Avebury, other than in the development of farms and extensive field systems on the Marlborough Downs. Hill forts such as Oldbury to the west and Barbury to the north, dominated the Iron Age landscape. Roman activity in the area is most clearly shown by the Roman road (A4), that once connected Mildenhall with Bath. Parts of the Roman road can still be seen, especially on the south side of the Devizes road (A4361). The Romans used Silbury Hill to line up the road, and there were small farmsteads and villas dotted across the landscape. The Saxons (cAD600–1066) also came to Avebury. They used Silbury as some sort of stronghold or lookout and settled inside the circle of Avebury itself. The place was called Waledich, or *Weala-dic* ('the dyke of the Britons') and the name is of Saxon derivation. The Circle formed a convenient semi-fortified site for a village. Settlements extended outside the bank and ditch to the west and by the Kennet stream, where earthworks can still be seen. It is thought that the stones of Avebury have remained undisturbed

Skeleton of barber-surgeon found in 1938 under stone 9. In his purse were scissors and coins

until this time, although many may have fallen.

Medieval Avebury

The ancient and curious stones of Avebury were probably the focus of pagan beliefs and cults that had survived. The fast-growing influence of the medieval church may well have found the rival cults associated with the stones too serious a threat, and a programme of destruction was organised. The stones were systematically buried.

The best evidence for the medieval destruction of Avebury was the finding in 1938 of the skeleton of a barber-surgeon under stone 9 in the south-west sector. This individual had accidentally been crushed under the falling stone in *c*AD1310-20.

The presence of the Church at Avebury was considerable. First a Saxon church was built right outside the banks of the pagan henge, and traces of this early church can still be seen in the internal fabric, with small round windows on the north wall of the nave, and other decorated fragments of Saxon type. An early twelfth-century Benedictine cell was

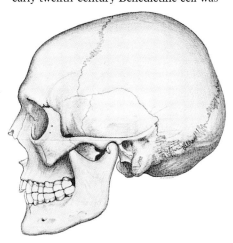

Drawing of the barber-surgeon's skull. His neck and pelvis were also broken

Stukeley's sketch of Avebury from the southern entrance in 1722. Fenced fields dissect the land

founded on the site of the present manor, and after it was dissolved in 1414, the church was further enlarged.

Comparable ecclesiastical pressure against the pagan circles can be seen at Knowlton in Dorset, where a medieval church was placed in the centre of the largest circle. In Brittany, there are records of the destruction of the standing stones of Carnac, or alternatively, the 'Christianisation' of stones with crosses placed on them.

Archaeological History

Avebury became the focus of antiquarian researches from 1649, when the famous antiquarian John Aubrey first 're-discovered' Avebury. Later, from 1719-24, William Stukeley recorded the stones and earthworks of the Avebury area during a period of rapid destruction. Throughout the nineteenth century, Avebury attracted all types of archae-ological research, but it was not until 1908–22 that serious and systematic excavation under the direction of H St G Gray took place. Gray excavated the ditch at Avebury and established the Neolithic date of the site. During the 1920s, Alexander Keiller bought Windmill Hill and began excavations there. It was the first causewayed enclosure in Britain to be properly excavated. Later, in 1934, he bought the Avenue, Avebury Circle, the manor and farm, and excavated and restored the sites until the outbreak of the Second World War in 1939. He also set up his Morven Institute of Archaeological Research in the stables of Avebury Manor and established the Museum which now bears his name.

The Sanctuary was located and excavated in 1930 by Maud Cunnington. In 1955–56, the West Kennet Long Barrow was excavated by Stuart Piggott and Richard Atkinson, and restored to its present state. Following the death of Al-

An excavated section through the great ditch at Avebury in 1922, showing its remarkable depth of 9m (30ft). Five seasons of work were organised by H St George Gray 1908—22

exander Keiller in 1955, Isobel Smith re-excavated at Windmill Hill, and obtained radiocarbon datings and environmental samples, using the new methods of modern archaeology. Silbury Hill was excavated under the direction of Richard Atkinson in 1968-69, with the BBC. A new tunnel was dug to investigate the mound, and it established the Neolithic date of the site and the three different phases of building. More recently, Cardiff University has conducted excavations directed towards interpreting the environmental changes in the prehistoric landscape of Avebury. Future work will examine the complete landscape and look for settlement and environmental traces threatened by modern agricultural methods.

One of the huge stones of the Avebury Circle being lifted and reset in 1938, during three seasons of excavation and restoration at Avebury by Alexander Keiller

ALEXANDER KEILLER MUSEUM

The Alexander Keiller Museum, located in an attractive stone coachouse behind the parish church in Avebury, houses an important collection of Neolithic material from the monuments.

Originally founded in 1935 by Alexander Keiller as his private museum for his personal archaeological collection, it was presented to the Ministry of Works in 1966 by Keiller's widow. The Museum is now managed by the National Trust.

The collection is predominantly made up of the artefacts excavated on Windmill Hill and within the Avebury Circle. A classic collection of Neolithic pottery is one of the chief treasures, together with a remarkable reference collection of Earlier

Neolithic flint tools, animal bones and artefacts.

The Barn gallery is an addition to the Museum from 2001. It contains the 'Avebury: 6000 years of mystery' exhibition, which covers development of the Avebury landscape, its many archaeological sites and more recent historical past over 6000 years. The exhibition includes objects from the collection, 'hands-on' interactives, models and computer-aided interactive displays.

The Museum staff are available to help with queries. There is also a Study Centre for visiting school and college groups, and educational material has been prepared to assist with projects.

FURTHER READING

BARKER, C T, 1984 The long mounds of the Avebury region. *Wiltshire Archaeological Magazine*, 79, 7-38

BRADLEY, R, 1984 *The Social Foundations of Prehistoric Britain*, London (Longman)

BURGESS, C, 1980 *The Age of Stonehenge* London (Dent)

BURL, A, 1979 *Prehistoric Avebury*. New Haven (Yale University Press)

CUNNINGTON, M, 1931 The Sanctuary on Overton Hill, near Avebury. *Wilts. Archaeological Mag*, 45: 300-35

DARVILLE, T, 1987 *Prehistoric Britain*. London (Batsford)

GRAY, H ST G, 1935 The Avebury Excavations, 1908-22. *Archaeologia 84*

HUNTER, M, 1982 *John Aubrey and the Realm of Learning*. London (Duckworth)

MALONE, C, 1989 *The English Heritage Book of Avebury*. London (Batsford)

PIGGOTT, S, 1940 Timber Circles: A re-examination. *Arch journal 96*

PIGGOTT, S, 1962 *The West Kennet Long Barrow*. London (HMSO)

PIGGOTT, S, 1985 *William Stukeley: an eighteenth-century antiquary*. London (Thames and Hudson)

SIMPSON, D A AND MEGAW, V, 1979 *An Introduction to British Prehistory*. Leicester University Press

SMITH, I F, 1965 *Windmill Hill and Avebury: Excavations by Alexander Keiller 1925-39*. Oxford (Clarendon Press)

SMITH, R W, 1984 The ecology of Neolithic farming systems as exemplified by the Avebury region of Wiltshire. *Proceedings of the Prehistoric Society*, 50: 99-120

WHITTLE, A, AND THOMAS, J, 1986 Anatomy of a tomb: West Kennet revisited. *Oxford journal of Archaeology*, 5, 127-56.

GLOSSARY

Avenue   Processional or ceremonial way, marked by standing stones, posts or linear earthworks leading from the entrance of a henge monument or stone circle

Barrow, Long   Neolithic burial tomb, elongated, with an entrance. Made of earth, chalk and stone. Some had burial chambers built of megalithic stones. The barrows were used for successive interments over many generations. Grave goods were simple flint and stone tools and pottery

Barrow, Round   Dating from the final Neolithic or Bronze Age, the barrows were circular in form, often with a surrounding ditch or bank. They normally contained a primary burial with one or more burials, or cremations (in urns). Grave goods were pots, stone and metal tools, jewellery and sometimes gold

Beaker Culture Named after the beaker-shaped pots found in burials and settlements in the final Neolithic (or copper age) and the Earlier Bronze Age. Found throughout Europe from c2400 to 1900BC, the beakers were found with a typical assemblage consisting of flint arrowheads and scrapers, copper daggers, stone buttons and wrist guard, and may have been part of a warrior's kit. Often called Beaker people, the makers of Beaker pottery also were the first users of metal

Berm   The flat 'shelf' area between the inner bank and ditch of a henge, that stopped excess soil falling from the bank into the ditch

Bronze Age   Prehistoric period following the Neolithic, c1800-700BC, when bronze tools and weapons were in use. The final Beaker culture and the Wessex culture both fall within the Bronze Age

Causeway Enclosure   Traditionally called 'camps', causewayed enclosures were Earlier Neolithic hill-top sites, enclosed by ditches and interrupted by causewayed entrances. The enclosures may have been used for settlement, ceremonial and economic purposes, and were in use from c3500 to 2800BC

Corbelling   In megalithic tombs a method of supporting a roof using overlapping wall slabs crowned with a single capstone

Cove   A setting of standing stones at centre of stone circle or in stone alignment

Cursus   Parallel earth banks or pits of Earlier Neolithic date, often extending for considerable distances. The purpose is unknown but is connected with the use of long barrows and henge monuments

Emmer and Einkorn Wheat   Early cultivated varieties of wheat, originating from the Near East. Introduced to Britain in the Neolithic and replaced by genetically improved varieties such as spelt and bread wheat in the Late Bronze Age and Iron Age

Flint   Formed of silica nodules found in cretaceous chalk. Flint was used in prehistoric tools. Flint nodules were mined and, when 'knapped', flakes formed sharp cutting edges. They could also be polished into axe heads

Henge Monument   Neolithic ceremonial circular enclosure, surrounded by a bank and ditch, with one or more causeway entrances. Internal features included settings of standing stones or wooden posts, pits and circular buildings

Megalithic   Literally, 'of large stones'; figuratively, of the culture or period

Neolithic   Period of prehistory, meaning the New Stone Age, which followed the Mesolithic or Middle Stone Age. Beginning in Britain after *c*4500BC and marked by the introduction of agriculture, domestic animals, cereals, pottery and ground stone tools. Followed by the Bronze Age *c*1900BC

Oolitic   Form of Jurassic limestone rock, composed of small corals

Quern   Stone used for grinding corn. Made of rough sandstone or other hard rock, such as sarsen, and shaped into concave saddle shapes in the Neolithic and more elaborate forms in later times

Radiocarbon Dating   Method of dating organic material. All living organisms during life absorb the isotope C14, which decays at a constant rate after death. Following special laboratory mea-surements, the age of the material can be calculated in radiocarbon years. The readings are then 'calibrated' to calendar years using conversion tables compiled from comparative tree growth-ring analysis. Radiocarbon dates are published as bc, or 'before calibration', and BC for calendar years

Sarsen   A hard sandstone rock derived from a silicaceous sand formed above cretaceous chalk about 30–20 million years ago. After geological upheavals, the sarsen was broken into small blocks and deposited over the chalk downs, and washed into the surrounding valleys. During the Neolithic, some sarsen stones were selected for erecting as standing stones, and were hauled into position at Avebury, West Kennet Long Barrow and Stonehenge, using ropes and rollers of wooden logs

Tranchet   Chisel edge of flint axe or arrowhead, made by flaking

Wessex Culture   The Wessex Culture dates from *c*1700 to 1200BC and is represented mainly by the rich grave goods of metal, amber and gold in round barrows. The final phase of Stonehenge was constructed during the Wessex Culture period